Way to Be!

Way to Be!

NINE WAYS TO BE HAPPY AND
MAKE SOMETHING OF YOUR LIFE

GORDON B. HINCKLEY

Foreword by Steve Young

Simon & Schuster

SIMON & SCHUSTER and colophon are registered trademarks of
Simon & Schuster, Inc.

For information regarding special discounts for bulk purchases,
please contact Simon & Schuster Special Sales:
1-800-456-6798 or business@simonandschuster.com.

Designed by Publications Development Company of Texas.

Manufactured in the United States of America

10   9   8   7   6   5   4   3   2   1

Library of Congress Cataloging-in-Publication Data is available.

ISBN 0-7432-3830-3

Dedicated to a generation of young people
who will rise to meet the exciting opportunities
of a new and challenging day.

From my experience, life is a lot like football. I can tell you from painful personal experience that throwing an interception on *Monday Night Football* with 80,000 fans screaming at you in the stadium and millions more watching on television is embarrassing and depressing. The boos from the crowd ring in your ears. Your teammates look at you as if you had just stolen their lunch. At those moments, you just want to dig a hole and disappear.

I am sorry to say that I have thrown my share of interceptions. But there is good reason for that. The big guys who are charging after you make it pretty impossible to see what's going on downfield.

If you want to be a good quarterback, you have to be willing and able to throw the ball blind. If you wait to see the receiver before you throw, it is almost always too late, and chances are you will end up on your backside looking at the stars and enduring the taunting of the crowd.

In order to have the courage to throw the football blind, I needed to have the faith that all the hours of practice, all the accumulated game-day experience, and all the mentoring from my coaches would help me know when and where to throw it. I had to believe that if I followed the fundamentals of good quarterbacking that my coaches had taught me, the ball would usually go where I wanted it to go.

If we are going to play the game of life, we can assume that we're going to throw a few interceptions, or make a few mistakes, from time to time. Often we face situations in which it feels as though we are throwing blind—we must make decisions without knowing exactly what the consequences will be. But if we have good coaches to mentor us and teach us the fundamentals, and good friends to help us keep track of what we've learned, we are in a much better position to make the right moves.

Way to Be! is more important than any playbook I ever had in the NFL, because it will help you avoid life's fumbles and interceptions. And that is because it is counsel from someone who is wise, someone who has your best interests at heart, someone who wants only for you to be happy and find true joy. It is like getting plays called in from the sidelines by an exceptional coach who knows which plays to call when the going gets tough and the game is on the line.

Gordon B. Hinckley is not just a wise and just man, though he is certainly that. He is a respected world religious leader and for me the ultimate earthly coach, whose counsel emphasizes the fundamentals that will help us all win the game of life.

Steve Young

CONTENTS

CONTENTS

Way to Be!

INTRODUCTION

There never was a time such as this. What a season in the history of the world to be alive! Never before has there been such a generation of youth.

Of course there are problems—not just a few. There are the dropouts, the deadbeats, the indolent, the failures. But even these can be reclaimed. But more important, there are great numbers of bright and able young men and women who wish to make something good of their lives.

You really are "a chosen generation." You are better educated. You desire to do the right thing. Many of you are trying to keep yourselves free from the corrosive stains of the world. In so many ways, you are remarkable! You are exceptional! I believe that as a group, you are the finest this world has ever seen.

It is important for you to understand that you are part of a chosen generation. Limitless is your potential. Magnificent is your future, if you will take control of it and if you will decide now that you will not let your life drift in a fruitless and aimless manner.

I am now old in years—90 plus. I have lived a long time, and I have lived with great love for the young men and young women of this world. What a truly wonderful group you are. You speak various languages. You are all part of a great family. But you are also individuals, each with his or her problems, each wishing for answers to the things that perplex and worry you. How I love you and long constantly for the genius to help you. Your lives are filled with difficult decisions and with dreams and hopes to find that which will bring you peace and happiness.

Once upon a very long time ago, I was your age. I didn't worry about drugs or pornography because they were not available then. I worried about school and where it would lead. It was the season of the terrible economic depression. I worried about how to earn a living. When I finished the university, I went to England. We traveled by train to Chicago, made a bus transfer across that city, and went on to New York, where we caught a steamship for the British Isles. While riding the transfer bus in Chicago, a woman said to the driver, "What is that building ahead?" He said, "Ma'am, that is the Chicago Board of Trade Building. Every week some man who has lost his fortune jumps out of one of those windows because he has nothing left to live for."

Such were the times. They were mean and ugly. No one who did not live through that period will ever understand it fully. I hope with all my heart we never have anything like it again. I mention this only to explain that I have lived through some challenging times in my life, and I know what it is to worry about the future and to wonder what it may hold.

Now, here you are on the threshold of your mature life. You may worry about school. You may worry about marriage. You may worry about the violence that seems to be all around us. You may worry about how you will earn a living. You may worry about being left behind in the hunt for prosperity. You may worry about many things.

Nonetheless, this is the age of great opportunity. You are so fortunate to be alive. Never in the history of mankind has life been filled with so many opportunities and challenges. When I was born in 1910, the average lie expectancy of a man or woman in the United States and other Western countries was fifty years. Now it is more than seventy-five years. Can you imagine that? On average you may expect to live at least twenty-five years longer than someone who lived in 1910.

This is the season of an explosion of knowledge. In my childhood and youth, there were no antibiotics. All of these wonderful medicines have been discovered and refined in more recent times. Some of the great scourges of the earth are gone.

Smallpox once took whole populations. That is gone. It is a miracle. Polio was once the dreaded fear of every mother. I recall going to visit a man with polio in the county hospital. He was in a large iron lung that pumped air into his lungs, allowing him to breathe. There was no hope for him; he couldn't breathe on his own. He died, leaving his wife and children. This terrible disease has almost disappeared. That too is a miracle. Cancer is now the target of scores of research centers. Its cure will surely come before long.

Of course you face challenges. Every generation that has walked the earth has faced challenges. But of all the challenges that have been faced in the past, the ones we have today, I believe, are the most easily handled. You may be surprised that I say that, for so many of the commentators and nay-sayers we see regularly on television and in the news shout that society's problems have never been worse than they are today. I don't believe it. The problems of today are manageable. They largely involve individual behavioral decisions, but those decisions can be made and followed. And when that happens, the challenge is behind us.

This is one reason I say that you of this chosen generation cannot simply sit idly by and let the world drift along its aimless way. It needs your strength, your courage, your voice in speaking up for those values that can save it and make it better.

None has a more compelling responsibility and opportunity than do you; for the future—of the family you will have, of the community and even the nation in which you live—is in your hands. You are young. You have energy. You have convictions in your heart. You have years yet to live. You have associates and friends with whom you can work.

You are good. But it is not enough just to be good. You must be good for something. You must contribute good to the world. The world must be a better place for your presence. And the good that is in you must be spread to others.

I do not suppose that any of us will be remembered a thousand years from now. I do not suppose that we will be remembered a century from now. But in this world so filled with problems, so constantly threatened by dark and evil challenges, you can and must rise above mediocrity, above indifference. You can become involved and speak with a strong voice for that which is right.

Not long ago someone gave me a copy of my old high school yearbook. I spent an hour thumbing through it, looking at the pictures of my friends who comprised my high school graduating class, the class of 1928. I looked at the faces of the boys who were my friends. Once they were young and bright and energetic. Now those few who are left are wrinkled and slow in their walk. I looked at the faces of the girls I knew. Many of them who were once so attractive have passed on, and the remainder live in the shadows of life. 1928 had its season of high hopes and splendid dreams.

In our quieter moments, we were all dreamers. The boys dreamed of mountains yet to climb and careers yet to be lived and fortunes yet to be made and families yet to rear. The girls dreamed of becoming mothers, of accomplishing some kind of great good in the world around them, and of becoming the kind of woman that most of them saw in their mothers.

I am sure it is the same for each of us, for you who find yourself today where I and my friends found ourselves more than seventy years ago.

How, then, can you become the man or woman you dream of becoming?

I hope that you are studying diligently and that your great ambition is to get A grades in your various courses. I hope your teachers will be generous toward you and that your studies will yield an excellent education. I could wish nothing better for you in your schoolwork.

I am going to be content to let your instructors give you the A's that I hope you will earn. I wish to give you some B's, or perhaps more correctly, some "Ways to Be!" You keep working for the A's, and in these pages I will give you the B's. They are Be's that I believe will make your life better, fuller, and more satisfying. They are the Be's that I have come to believe through all these years, form a template for success—for anyone's success. They are nine Be's, nine suggestions gleaned from more than nine decades of living, that will help you achieve happiness and success.

First, Be Grateful.

Second, Be Smart.

Third, Be Involved.

Fourth, Be Clean.

Fifth, Be True.

Sixth, Be Positive.

Seventh, Be Humble.

Eighth, Be Still.

And Ninth, Be Prayerful.

1
BE GRATEFUL

B E GRATEFUL.

There are two little words in the English language that perhaps mean more than all others. They are "thank you." Comparable words are found in *every* other language—*gracias, merci, danke, obrigado, domo,* and so forth.

In my boyhood home, my parents devoted a particular evening every week to spending time with the family. During our home evening together, we would do many things, including performing for one another. We were miserable performers. For one of us children to sing a solo was like asking ice cream to stay hard on the kitchen stove. We would laugh and make cute and comical (or so we thought) remarks about one another's performance. But our parents persisted. They were determined that our family spend time with each other—even if our musical ability left something to be desired. So we sang together. We prayed together. We listened quietly while mother read stories to us. And we enjoyed the stories our father told us out of his memory. Our father was an excellent storyteller, and I still remember some of the tales he told. One of those stories went like this:

An older boy and his young companion were walking along a road that led through a field. They saw an old coat and a badly worn pair of men's shoes by the roadside, and in the distance they saw the owner working in the field.

The younger boy suggested that they hide the shoes, conceal themselves, and watch the perplexity on the owner's face when he returned.

The older boy thought that would not be so good. He said the owner must be a very poor man. So, after talking the matter over, at his suggestion, they decided to try another experiment. Instead of hiding the shoes, they would put a silver dollar [which was then a commonly used coin] in each shoe and see what the owner did when he discovered the money.

Pretty soon the man returned from the field, put on his coat, slipped one foot into a shoe, felt something hard, took his foot out and found the silver dollar. Wonder and surprise shone upon his face. He looked at the dollar again and again, turned around and could see nobody, then proceeded to put on the other shoe. When to his great surprise he found another dollar, his feelings overcame him. He knelt down and offered aloud a prayer of thanksgiving, in which he spoke of his wife being sick and helpless and his children without bread. He fervently thanked the Lord for this bounty from unknown hands and evoked the blessing of heaven upon those who gave him this needed help.

The boys remained hidden until he had gone. They had been touched by his prayer and by his sincere expression of gratitude. As they left to walk down the road, one said to the other, "Don't you have a good feeling?" (Adapted from Bryant S. Hinckley, *Not by Bread Alone*, Bookcraft, 1955, p. 95.)

Gratitude creates the most wonderful feeling. It can resolve disputes. It can strengthen friendships. And it makes us better men and women.

The habit of saying thank you is the mark of a cultivated mind. With whom is the Lord displeased? Those who do not confess his hand in all things. That is, those who are not grateful for all that they have and all they are. So my first suggestion to you, my dear young friends, is that you walk with gratitude in your hearts. Be thankful for the wonderful blessings that are yours. Be grateful for the tremendous opportunities that you have. Be thankful to your parents, who care so very much about you and who have worked so very hard to provide for you. Say thank you to your mother and your father who love you and make it possible for you to do so many things. In most cases, there are no two people who care more about you than do your parents. Say thank you to your grandparents and your aunts and uncles who often go out of their way to make your life better. Say thank you to your friends. Say thank you to the neighbor next door who is understanding when you shoot baskets way past dark or accidently trample his flowerbed. Express appreciation to everyone who does you a favor or assists you in any way. You will be surprised how often you find yourself saying simply, "Thank you."

Thank the Lord for His goodness to you. Shakespeare said, "O Lord, that lends me life, lend me a heart replete with thankfulness." (*King Henry VI*, Part 2, I.i. 19–20.) Thank Him for His great example, for His tremendous teachings, for His outreaching hand. Read about Him and read His words. Read them quietly to yourself and then ponder them. Pour out your heart to your Father in Heaven with gratitude for the gift of His Beloved Son.

Thank Him for friends and loved ones, for parents and brothers and sisters, for family. Thank him for a strong body, for a sound mind, for teachers who guide you and mentors who take a special interest in you, for those willing to coach you and help you develop new talents or become better at something you love.

Thank Him that you live in a land of freedom where you can come and go as you please and make choices that suit you. Thank Him that you live in a time of relative prosperity. Thank Him for the advances in communication that allow you to stay close to those you love and interact almost instantly with people half way around the world. Thank Him for the ease of travel and the privilege of getting an education. And yes, even thank Him for your struggles, for they will make you strong—if you will let them. You will find people responding to you differently than they have before. And interestingly, you will find that you are happier than you have been. Your gratitude will encourage others to be grateful in return.

Your very attitude toward life can be evidence of whether or not you are truly grateful for life, for the blessings you have, for the comforts and privileges and opportunities you enjoy, for the talents you have been given, for everything.

Be grateful. Count your blessings and gifts and privileges and see just how long that list is. I imagine that each of you will have difficulties ahead of you. None of us can avoid them. But do not despair. Do not give up. Look for the sunlight in the clouds. And be grateful for what you have.

Try to be grateful even when you encounter challenges and problems along the way of life, because you will. Like everyone else, you will have difficulties to overcome. But they will not last forever. And God will not forsake you.

Let a spirit of thanksgiving guide and bless your days and nights. Work at it. You will find that it will yield wonderful results.

2

BE SMART

SECOND, BE SMART.

You are moving into the most competitive age the world has ever known. All around you is competition. You need all the education you can get. Sacrifice a car, if necessary, sacrifice anything that is needed to be sacrificed to qualify yourselves to do the work of the world. That world will, in large measure, pay you what it thinks you are worth, and your worth will increase as you gain education and proficiency in your chosen field.

Train your mind and your hands to become an influence for good as you go forward with your life. And as you do so and as you perform with excellence, you will bring honor to yourself and to your family. You will be regarded as a man or woman of integrity and ability and conscientious workmanship. Be smart. Don't be foolish. You cannot bluff or cheat others without bluffing or cheating yourself.

By suggesting that you be smart, I do not mean smart-alecky or anything of that kind. I mean, be wise. Be intelligent. Be smart about training yourself for the future. Be wise about preparing for what lies ahead.

Many years ago, I worked for a railroad in the central offices in Denver, Colorado. I was in charge of what is called head-end traffic. That was in the days when nearly everyone rode passenger trains. One morning I received a call from my counterpart in Newark, New Jersey. He said, "Train number such-and-such has arrived, but it has no baggage car. Somewhere, 300 passengers have lost their baggage, and they are mad."

I went immediately to work to find out where it may have gone. I found it had been properly loaded and properly trained in Oakland, California. It had been moved to our railroad in Salt Lake City, been carried to Denver, down to Pueblo, put on another line, and moved to St. Louis. There it should have been handled by another railroad which would take it to Newark, New Jersey. But some thoughtless switchman in the St. Louis yards moved a small piece of steel just three inches, a switch point, then pulled the lever to uncouple the car. We discovered that a baggage car that belonged in Newark, New Jersey, was in fact in New Orleans, Louisiana—1,500 miles from its destination. The three-inch movement of the switch in the St. Louis yard by a careless employee had started it on the wrong track, and the distance from its true destination increased dramatically.

That is the way it is with our lives. Instead of following a steady course, we are pulled by some mistaken idea in another direction. The movement away from our original destination may be ever so small, but, if continued, that very small movement becomes a great gap, and we find ourselves far from where we intended to go.

Have you ever looked closely at one of those 16-foot farm gates? When it is opened, it swings very wide. The end at the hinges moves ever so slightly, while out at the perimeter the movement is great. It is usually the little things that make the big difference in our lives.

Be smart. Prepare. Be a good student in school. Resist thinking that what you do now doesn't matter, because it does. The pattern of study you establish during your formal schooling will in large measure affect your lifelong thirst for knowledge. There are few things more pathetic than those who have lost their curiosity and sense of adventure, and who no longer care to learn.

Education is a shortcut to proficiency. It makes it possible to leapfrog over the mistakes of the past. It makes it possible to excel and advance more quickly. Regardless of the vocation you choose, you can speed your journey in getting there through education. So be smart about being smart. Don't forfeit the schooling that will enhance your future in order to satisfy your desire for immediate, fleeting pleasure. Cultivate the long view of life. You are going to be around for a good while.

You don't have to be a genius to do great things. The important work of this world is done, for the most part, by ordinary people who do their work in an extraordinary way.

It matters not whether you choose to be a businessman, a professor, a carpenter, a computer programmer, a doctor, or to follow any other honorable vocation. The important thing is that you qualify to be useful to society. It is so easy and yet so tragic to become a drifter or a druggie or a dropout. On the other hand, it is so challenging and so satisfying to be a producer and a builder—of not only buildings or careers, but lives.

The Savior, who is the perfect example in all things, is a model for growing intellectually. In one of the few verses that gives us insight into the time between when as a boy He was found teaching His elders in the temple and His formal ministry, we learn that He "increased in wisdom and stature, and in favour with God and man" (Luke 2:52). In other words, even the Savior had to learn and grow and progress in wisdom—to grow intellectually.

So be smart. Don't be foolish.

It is not only in getting an education that you need to be smart. Be smart in your appearance and in your manners. I am not suggesting that you need to go about dressed like a fashion model. I am suggesting that you be clean and neat in your appearance, that you be gentle in your speech, that you be courteous and respectful in your manner. So many people in our society today are sloppy in the way they look and in the way they behave. Sloppy dress signals sloppy ways and sloppy thinking.

As a boy, our parents insisted that we dress neatly for school. No untidy appearance was tolerated. The boys wore a shirt and tie and short trousers. We wore long black stockings that reached from the foot to above the knees. They were made of cotton and wore out quickly, so they had to be darned frequently. Even we boys learned how to darn because it was unthinkable to go to school with a hole in our stockings.

I realize those days are long gone. But they taught us something. We learned a lesson on the importance of being tidy and clean, a lesson that has blessed my life ever since. Because if we are neat and tidy in small ways, those habits carry over into larger areas of concern that have much greater and more long-lasting impact. Just as sloppy dress signals sloppy ways and sloppy thinking, a neat and well-groomed appearance indicates competence and dependability.

So again, I suggest that you Be Smart. Learn from other's successes as well as their mistakes. Prepare and school yourself for what lies ahead. Educate your minds and hands, whatever your interests or your chosen field. Whether it be repairing broken computers or repairing defective hearts, you must train yourself. Seek for the best schooling available. Become a workman of integrity in the world that lies ahead. You will bring honor to yourself and to your family, and you will be generously rewarded because of that training.

There can be no doubt, none whatever, that education pays. Do not short-circuit your education. If you do, you will pay for it over and over again.

3
BE INVOLVED

THIRD, BE INVOLVED.

When I say Be Involved, I am suggesting that you Be Involved in good works. Or, in other words, be willing to work.

In my boyhood home, we had a stove in the kitchen and a stove in the dining room. A furnace was later installed, and it was a wonderful thing on those cold winter nights. But it had a voracious appetite for coal, and there was no automatic stoker. The coal had to be shoveled into the furnace and carefully banked each night. That furnace taught us a great lesson: If you wanted to keep warm, you had to work the shovel.

My father had the idea that his boys ought to learn to work all year around, so he bought a fruit farm where we lived in the summer. We had a large orchard and the trees had to be pruned each spring, so our father took us to pruning demonstrations put on by experts from the state agricultural college. We learned a great truth there—that you could pretty well determine the kind of fruit you would pick in September by the way you pruned in February. I learned firsthand that what you sow you reap, that if we did our work well in the spring, we could expect a plentiful harvest in the fall. And naturally, the reverse was also true. If our work was careless in the spring, we suffered come harvest time.

Most of us tend to be inherently lazy. We would rather play than work. We would rather loaf than work. A little play and a little loafing are good from time to time. But it is work that spells the difference in the life of a young man or young woman. It is usually work and effort that explain the difference between the gold-medal athlete and those who finish even a fraction of a second later. It is work that provides the food we eat, the clothing we wear, the homes in which we live, the grades and training we receive. It is work that gives us a feeling of accomplishment. And it is work that allows us to feel that we are making a difference in the world.

My father had a horse and buggy when I was a boy. Then one summer day in 1916, a wonderful, almost magical thing happened. He came home driving a brand-new, shiny black Model T Ford. At the time it was regarded as a wonderful machine, but by today's standards it was crude and temperamental. For instance, it did not have a self-starter. It had to be cranked.

We quickly learned something about cranking that car. Either you retarded the spark, or the crank would kick back and break your hand. But the most interesting thing was the lights. The car had no storage battery. The only electricity came from what was called a magneto. The output of the magneto was determined by the speed of the engine. If the engine was running fast, the lights were bright. If the engine slowed, the lights became a sickly yellow. If you wanted to see ahead as you were going down the road, you had to keep the engine running at a fast clip.

As I have grown older, I have learned that it is the same for each of us. You have to stay on your feet and keep moving if you are going to have light in your life.

Nothing of real substance comes without work. Various periods of this earth's history have been denoted as ages, such as the age of stone, the age of fire, the age of industry, and so on. Someone has described ours as the age of fun, and the fact is that more money and more time are spent in trying to satisfy the physical desire for pleasure than ever before in the history of mankind.

I am not adverse to recreation. All work and no play makes Jack a dull boy and Jill a dull girl. But when play becomes the end in itself, then we are in danger.

I had a grade school friend whom I'll call Lynn. Lynn was always in trouble. He seemed to have a difficult time buckling down and doing any schoolwork, particularly when spring came and things looked better outside than in. He was the bane of our teacher's life. One day at about eleven o'clock, Lynn disturbed the class, and our teacher told him to go shut himself in the closet until she let him out. Lynn obediently went to the closet and closed the door behind him. When the bell rang at twelve o'clock, Lynn came out chewing the last bite of our teacher's lunch. We couldn't help laughing, all but our teacher, and that made matters worse. Lynn went on clowning most of his life. He never learned how to concentrate on what was going on. He never learned how to set his mind to a task. He never learned how to work. And sadly, he never really knew the sense of accomplishment that comes from a job well done.

It has been said that the north wind made the Vikings. Likewise, only through labor do nations become stronger, cities more attractive, families more tightly knit, and lives more robust. There is no substitute under the heavens for good, old-fashioned work. Most of the good done in this world is accomplished by people who set their minds to something and work until it is done. Such is the process by which dreams become realities. It is the best antidote for worry and the best medicine for despair. It is the process that leads to dynamic achievement. It is the process by which we grow and progress. And it is the process that helps us feel good about who we are and who we are becoming.

The writer of Proverbs declared: "Seest thou a man diligent in his business? He shall stand before kings" (Proverbs 22:29).

So Be Involved. Be Involved in good works. Be willing to work, for it will make all the difference in your life.

4
BE CLEAN

FOURTH, BE CLEAN.

When I was a boy, most homes were heated with coal stoves. Black smoke belched from almost every chimney. As winter came to a close, black soot and grime were everywhere, both inside and outside of the house. There was a ritual through which we passed each year, and not a very pleasant one, as we viewed it. It involved every member of the family. It was known as spring cleaning. When the weather warmed after the long winter, a week or so was designated as cleanup time. It was usually when there was a holiday and included two Saturdays.

Mother ran the show. All of the curtains were taken down, and then they were carefully laundered. The windows were washed inside and out, and oh, what a job that was in our big two-story house. Wallpaper was on all of the walls, and Father would bring home numerous cans of wallpaper cleaner. The new cleaner was like bread dough, but it was a pretty pink in color when the container was opened. It had an interesting smell, a pleasant, refreshing smell that I can still remember these many years later. We all pitched in, including our father. We would knead the cleaning dough in our hands, climb a ladder, and begin on the high ceiling and then work down the walls. The dough was soon black from the dirt it lifted from the paper. It was a terrible task, very tiring, but the results were like magic. We would stand back and compare the dirty surface with the clean surface. It was amazing to us how much better the clean walls looked.

All of the carpets were taken up and dragged out to the backyard, where they were hung over the clothesline, one by one. Each of us boys would have what we called a carpet beater, which was a device made of light steel rods with a wooden handle. As we beat the carpet, the dust would fly, and we would have to keep going until there was no dust left. We detested that work. But when all of it was done, and everything was back in place, the result was wonderful. The house was clean, our spirits renewed, and the whole world looked better.

Everything does look better when it's clean. And that includes us and the way we live our lives. During my boyhood, people got sick just as they get sick now, though I believe that more people became sick more often back in those days. When someone was diagnosed as having chicken pox or measles, the doctor would advise the city health department, and a man would be sent to put up a sign in the front window. This was a warning to any who might wish to come inside that they did so at their own peril. If the disease was smallpox or diphtheria, the sign was bright orange with black letters that said, in effect, "Stay away from this place."

Thus we learned that things look and feel better when they're clean, and to stay away from areas that were not clean. Those practices have served me well, for we live in a world that is filled with filth and sleaze, a world that reeks of evil. It is all around us. It is on the television screen. It is at the movies. It is in the popular literature. It is on the Internet. It is in the lyrics of popular songs. It is available through the telephone. You can't afford to watch or listen to it. You cannot afford to let that filthy poison touch you. Stay away from it. Avoid it. Shun it like the plague. You can't rent videos that portray degrading things without expecting to have them affect you in destructive ways.

Avoid evil talk. Do not take the name of the Lord in vain. From the thunders of Sinai the finger of the Lord wrote on tablets of stone, "Thou shalt not take the name of the Lord thy God in vain" (Exodus 20:7). It is not a mark of manhood to carelessly and disrespectfully use the name of the Almighty or His Beloved Son in a vain and flippant way, as many are prone these days to do. Such language only marks you as someone who has no respect for anything sacred. Profanity is the sign of an uneducated, uncultured, careless man or woman.

I will never forget coming home from school one day, throwing my books on the table, and taking the name of the Lord in vain as I expressed relief that school was out for the day. Mother heard me and was shocked. She took me by the hand and led me to the bathroom. There she got a clean washcloth and a clean bar of soap. She told me to open my mouth, then proceeded to wash my mouth with that terrible soap. I blubbered and protested. She stayed at it for a long time and then said, "Don't let me ever hear such words from your lips again."

The taste was terrible. The reprimand was worse. I have never forgotten it.

I had a dear friend, a man I admired immensely, who underwent many surgeries. On one occasion as he was being wheeled out of the operating room, the attendant pushing the gurney stumbled and let out an oath using the name of the Lord. My friend, who was still somewhat under anesthesia, managed to say weakly, "Please! Please! That is my Lord whose name you revile." There was a deathly silence, and then the young man whispered with a subdued voice, "I'm sorry."

I have never forgotten that lesson, which leads me to urge you to choose your friends carefully. It is they who will lead you in one direction or the other. Everybody wants friends. Everybody needs friends. No one wishes to be without them. But never lose sight of the fact that it is your friends who will lead you along the paths that you will follow. While you should be friendly with all people, select with great care those whom you wish to have close to you. They will be your safeguards in situations where you may vacillate between choices, and you in turn may save them.

Be clean. Don't waste your time or your money on destructive entertainment. I have been told about the filthy, lascivious shows put on by performing groups of various kinds. The young people of countless communities pay large sums of money to get in. What do they get for their money? Only seductive voices urging them to move in the direction of the slimy, salacious things of life. I plead with you to stay away from such trash. It will not help you. It can only injure you.

I am concerned about some trends that seem to have infiltrated our society, and in a particular way large numbers of youth. I recognize that mentioning these trends will be unpopular with some and considered totally out-of-touch by others, but I do it as one who has seen many trends come and go.

One of the trends I wish to mention involves tattoos. Without exception, the tattoos that cover large portions of the arms, legs, and even face and neck, are hideous.

I am puzzled by this trend, that seems to have overtaken so many. What creation is more magnificent than the human body? What a wondrous thing it is as the crowning work of the Almighty. Paul, in writing to the Corinthians, said: "Know ye not that ye are the temple of God, and that the Spirit of God dwelleth in you? If any man defile the temple of God, him shall God destroy; for the temple of God is holy, which temple ye are" (1 Corinthians 3:16–17).

Have you ever thought about your body as being holy? Have you ever thought about it being like a temple? Have you ever stopped to think that your body is a gift from God?

You are a child of God. Your body is His creation. Would you disfigure that creation with portrayals of people, animals, and words painted into your skin? Even worse, would you disfigure your body with seductive scenes and words?

I promise you that the time will come, if you have tattoos, that you will regret your actions. They are permanent. Only by an expensive and painful process can they be removed. If you are tattooed, then probably for the remainder of your life you will carry it with you. I believe the time will come when it will be an embarrassment to you. I plead with you to avoid it.

Another trend has to do with earrings and rings placed in other parts of the body. These are not manly. They are not attractive. Young men look better without them, and I believe they feel better without them. As for young women, they do not need to drape rings up and down their ears. One pair of earrings is actually more beautiful than an array of metal that almost always detracts from the natural beauty of the face and hair. I mention these things because again they concern your body.

How truly beautiful is a well-groomed young woman who is clean in body and mind. She is a daughter of God in whom her Eternal Father can take pride. How handsome is a young man who is well groomed. He is a son of God in whom his Eternal Father can also take pride. He does not need tattoos or earrings on or in his body.

There are other threats to personal cleanliness. Over the years I have traveled to Asia many times. In the early sixties I had reason to visit the island of Okinawa frequently during a time when there were American servicemen stationed there in large numbers. Some of them had cars, many of which were badly rusted. There were holes in the fenders and in the side panels. Whatever paint was left was dull. All of this was the result of corrosive ocean salt in the air that ate through the metal.

That is the way pornography is. This sleazy filth is like corrosive salt. It will eat through your armor if you expose yourself to it. It will corrode your morals, your values, and your sense of self-worth. The makers and marketers of this slimy stuff grow wealthy while the character of their customers decays. The producers and purveyors of smut are assiduously working a mine that yields them many millions of dollars in profit. Their products are designed to titillate and stimulate the baser instincts. Many a man who has partaken of forbidden fruit and then discovered that he has destroyed his marriage, lost his self-respect, and broken his companion's heart, has come to realize that the booby-trapped jungle trail he has followed began with the reading or viewing of pornographic material. Some who would not think of taking a sip of liquor or using illicit drugs have rationalized indulgence in pornography.

Pornography has become a $10 billion industry in the United States, where a few men grow rich at the expense of thousands who are their victims. Stay away from it. It may at first seem exciting, but it will destroy you. It will warp your senses. It will distort your ideas about sex and love. It will build within you an appetite that you will do anything to appease. And don't try to create associations through the Internet and chat rooms. They can lead you down into an abyss of sorrow and bitterness.

Stay away from pornography as you would avoid a serious disease. In essence, place a bright orange warning sign with black letters in front of any source of sexually salacious material. Pornography will corrode your values and your morals just as surely as the sea breeze ate away those cars on Okinawa. Those who indulge in pornography get so they cannot leave it alone. It will enslave you.

Drugs will also enslave you. I don't care what the variety may be. They will destroy you if pursued. You will become their slave. Once in their power, you will do anything to get money to buy more.

I was amazed to learn that parents introduce drugs to their children in 20 percent of the cases. I cannot understand what I regard as the sheer stupidity of these parents. What future other than slavery for their children could they see in them? Illegal drugs will utterly destroy those who become addicted to them.

My advice, my pleading to you wonderful young men and women, is to stay entirely away from them. Don't even experiment with drugs. Look about you and see the effects they have had on others. Stay away from these mind-altering and habit-forming addictions. They will steal your money, your agency, your freedom to do as you wish, and in many cases, the future you might have had.

Now, please realize that those who indulge in pornography and drugs and other habit-forming and addictive substances such as alcohol will try to make you believe that you are living in the dark ages if you don't partake of these things. "For the drunkard and the glutton shall come to poverty; and drowsiness shall clothe a man with rags" (Proverbs 23:21).

So-called keg parties have become a big thing at graduation time. Is this the best way to celebrate the achievement of years of study? The drinking of alcohol, whether beer, wine, or whiskey, can become habit-forming and addictive. You do not need it. You are better off without it.

And likewise tobacco. What will it do for you? It will make of you a slave to its seductive grip. Once the habit becomes established, it is difficult to break. Medical research has unmistakably demonstrated that cigarette smoking shortens life. Cancer, emphysema, and other painful and serious illnesses result from cigarette use.

When I see a young man or a young woman smoking I can't help but think, "Can't they read? How foolish and short-sighted can they be?" Smoking is a dirty habit. It has no redeeming qualities.

Please know that there are thousands, even millions of youth, who refrain from these kinds of dangerous, deceptive, addictive activities. Many students are eager for top grades and to participate in extracurricular activities in school. Many come from homes where religion is practiced and a code of ethics and morality is observed. Many youth have never had a drink or experimented with drugs or participated in premarital, sexual activities.

I congratulate those of you who fall into this category for maintaining your self-control and regarding yourself with enough respect to not follow the crowd. I congratulate you on your strength and on standing by your convictions. You are not alone. You are simply being wise and doing what is right and smart and clean.

And now just a word on the most common and most difficult of all problems for many young men and young women to handle. It is the relationship that you have with one another. You are dealing with the most powerful and the most wonderful of human instincts. Only the will to live possibly exceeds it.

Will and Ariel Durrant after a lifetime of observing history wrote: "A youth boiling with hormones will wonder why he should not give full freedom to his sexual desires, and if he is unchecked by custom, morals, or laws, he may ruin his life before he matures sufficiently to understand that sex is a river of fire that must be banked and cooled by a hundred restraints if it is not to consume in chaos both the individual and the group" (*Lessons of History*, Simon and Schuster, 1968, 35–36).

The Lord has made us attractive one to each other for a great purpose. But this very attraction becomes a powder keg unless it is kept under control. It is beautiful when handled in the right way. It is deadly if it gets out of hand.

Those who indulge in sexual activity outside the bonds of marriage do irreparable damage to themselves and rob the one with whom they are involved of that which can never be restored. There is nothing clever about this kind of so-called conquest. It carries with it no laurels, no victories, no enduring satisfaction. It brings only shame, sorrow, regret—and often disease. Those who so indulge cheat themselves and rob another. In so doing, they affront their Father in Heaven, for they are children of God. I know that this is strong language, plainly spoken. But the trend of our times calls for strong language and plain words.

For these reasons, I advise against early dating—or at least the early dating of just one other person. This suggestion is not designed to hurt you in any way or to hamper your social activity.

Steady dating at an early age leads often to tragedy. Studies have shown that the longer a boy and girl date one another, the more likely they are to lose control and get themselves into trouble. It is far better to date a variety of companions until you are ready to marry. Have a wonderful time with your friends, but stay away from familiarity with each other. Keep your hands to yourself. It may not be easy, but it is possible.

Sexual sin is just that—sin! Our society, and in particular the media, have made it look glamorous, but it is not. Sex used in the wrong place and wrong time will always result in heartache, heartbreak, and unnecessary trouble. Well did Sir Galahad say, "My strength is as the strength of ten, because my heart is pure" (Alfred, Lord Tennyson, Sir Galahad [1842], st. 1). I believe it.

My dear young friends, in matters of sex you know what is right. You know when you are walking on dangerous ground, when it is so easy to stumble and slide into the pit of transgression. I plead with you to be careful, to stand safely back from the cliff of sin over which it is so easy to fall. Keep yourselves clean from the dark and disappointing evil of sexual transgression. Walk in the sunlight of that peace which comes from virtue.

Now, if you have stepped over the line and slipped along the way, don't give up hope. There is hope for you. There is repentance. And there is forgiveness. That process begins with prayer. Share your burden with God. Share your burden with your parents, if you can. And counsel with a religious leader, if you can. You will pay a price if you have slipped, but if you are willing to repent, there can be a good life ahead.

All of these challenges considered, I am not asking you to be a prude. I am asking only that you Be Clean. Avoiding these temptations is almost entirely a matter of self-discipline. You know what is right and wrong. When you find yourself slipping in the direction of that which you know is wrong, it may be difficult to stop and turn around. But it can be done. It has been done by millions just like you who experience the same emotional and physical appeals.

Be Clean. Be clean in every way. Some day you will meet the man or woman of your dreams. Be clean for the sake of your future companion. Be clean for the sake of your posterity. Be clean for the sake of your self-respect.

There is nothing in all this world as magnificent as virtue. It glows without tarnish. It is precious and beautiful. It is above price. It cannot be bought or sold. It is the fruit of self-mastery.

Delight in Being Clean. Relish the challenge of standing above and beyond the base trends of the world. You will never regret it.

5

BE TRUE

FIFTH, BE TRUE.

Said Shakespeare, "To thine own self be true, and it must follow, as the night the day, thou canst not be false to any man" (*Hamlet*, I, iii, 78–81).

During my first year in junior high an unthinkable thing happened. Though a new junior high building had been constructed and we were the first class to enter its doors, the building was not large enough, and so our seventh-grade class—the youngest class—was sent back to grade school for one additional year.

We were insulted. We were furious. We had already spent six grade-school years in that building, and we felt we deserved something better. We were older now. We were far above going back to school with the "little kids." The boys of the class met after school, and we decided we simply would not tolerate this kind of treatment. We were determined we would take matters into our own hands by going on strike.

The next day we did not show up at school. But we had no place to go. We couldn't stay home, because our mothers would ask questions. We didn't think of going downtown to a show, because in those days we had no money for that. We didn't think of going to the park because we were afraid we would be seen by Mr. Clayton, the truant officer. We didn't think of going out behind the school fence and telling shady stories because we didn't know any. We had never heard of such things as drugs or anything of the kind. So we just wandered around and wasted the day.

The next morning, the principal, Mr. Stearns, was at the front door of the school to greet us. His demeanor matched his name. He said some pretty straightforward things and then told us that we could not come back to school until we brought a note from our parents. That was my first experience with a lockout. Striking, he said, was not the way to settle a problem. We were expected to be responsible citizens, and if we had a complaint, we could come to the principal's office and discuss it.

There was only one thing to do—and that was to go home and get the note.

I remember walking sheepishly into the house. My mother asked me what was wrong. I told her what I had done the day before and that I now needed a note to take back to the principal. She wrote a note. It was very brief. It was the most stinging rebuke she ever gave me. It read as follows:

Dear Mr. Stearns,

Please excuse Gordon's absence yesterday. His action was simply an impulse to follow the crowd.

She signed it and handed it to me.

I have never forgotten my mother's note. Though I had been an active party to the action we had taken, I resolved then and there that I would never do anything on the basis of simply following the crowd. I determined then and there that I would make my own decisions on the basis of their merits and not be influenced by those around me. I decided that I would be true to whatever I believed to be right.

That decision has blessed my life countless times in countless ways, sometimes in very uncomfortable circumstances. It has kept me from doing some things which, if indulged in, could at worst have resulted in serious trouble, and at best would have cost me my self-respect.

Be True. Be true to who you are. Be true to the parents who are rearing you and caring for you. Be true to the family whose name you bear. Be true to the land and country you call home. Be true to those within your circle of friendship. And most of all, be true to yourself.

In my high school yearbook is a picture of a young woman. She was bright and effervescent and beautiful. She was a charmer. Life for her could be summed up in one short word—F-U-N. She dated the boys and danced away the nights, studying a little but not too much, just enough to get grades that would take her through graduation. She married a boy of her own kind. Alcohol took possession of her life. She could not leave it alone. She was a slave to it. Her body succumbed to its treacherous grip. Sadly, her life faded without achievement.

There is a picture of another girl in that yearbook. She was not particularly beautiful. But she had a wholesome look about her, a sparkle in her eyes, and a smile on her face. She was friendly to all. Everyone liked her. She knew why she was in school. She was there to learn. Yes, she knew how to have fun, but she also knew when to stop and put her mind on other things.

There was a boy in our school also. He had come from a small rural town. He had very little money. He brought lunch in a brown paper bag. He looked a little like the farm from which he had come. There was nothing especially handsome or dashing about him. He was a good student. He had set a goal for himself. It was a lofty goal, and at times appeared almost unattainable.

These two fell in love. People said, "What does he see in her?" Or, "What does she see in him?" But they each saw something wonderful in each other which no one else saw.

Upon graduating from the university, they married. They scrimped and worked. Money was hard to come by. He went on to graduate school. She continued to work for a time, and then their children came. She gave her attention to them. Somehow they survived. And over time, they flourished.

A few years ago I was riding a plane home from the East. It was late at night, and as I walked down the aisle in the semidarkness, I saw a woman asleep with her head on the shoulder of her husband. She awakened as I approached. I immediately recognized the girl and boy I had known in high school so long before. They were now approaching old age. She proudly told me that they were returning from the East, where he had gone to deliver a paper. There at a great convention he had been honored by his peers from across the nation.

I learned that they had given much service to their fellowmen through the years. By every measure they were successful. They had realized the lofty goals which they had set for themselves. They had been honored and respected and had made a tremendous contribution to the society of which they were a part. Together and individually they had exceeded their dreams.

As I returned to my seat on the plane, I thought of those two girls. The life of one had been spelled out in a three-letter word: *F-U-N*. It had been lived aimlessly, without stability, without contribution to society, without ambition. It had ended in misery and pain and disappointment and early death.

The life of the other had been difficult. It had meant scrimping and saving. It had meant working and struggling to keep going. It had meant simple food and plain clothing and a very modest apartment in the years of her husband's initial effort to get started in his profession. But out of that seemingly sterile soil there had grown a plant, yes, two plants, side by side, that blossomed and bloomed in a beautiful and wonderful way. As I pondered the conversation with these two old friends, I determined within myself to do a little better, to be a little more dedicated, to set my sights a little higher, to love my wife a little more dearly, to help her and treasure her and look after her.

Doing what is right and being true to what you believe to be right and good has implications in every arena. I think of the 1912 World Series. This game was played when I was only two years old, so I don't remember it. But I have read about it. It was a hard-fought, eight-game series with one of the games called at midnight due to darkness. Playing fields were not electrically lighted at that time. It was the last game and the score was tied 1–1. The Boston Red Sox were at bat, the New York Giants in the field. A Boston batter knocked a high-arching fly. Two New York players ran for it. Fred Snodgrass in center field signaled to his associate that he would take it. He came squarely under the ball, which fell into his glove. But the ball went right through his hand and fell to the ground. A howl went up in the stands. The roaring fans couldn't believe it. Snodgrass had dropped the ball. He had caught hundreds of fly balls before. He had made dozens of defensive plays in this series alone. But now, at this crucial moment, he dropped the ball. The New York Giants lost. The Red Sox won the series.

Snodgrass came back the following season and played brilliant ball for nine more years. He lived to be eighty-six years of age. But after that one slip, for sixty-two years when he was introduced to anybody, he came to expect the response to be, "Oh, yes, you're the one who dropped the ball."

This phenomenon is not peculiar to sports. It happens every day in life.

There is the student who thinks he is doing well enough, and then under the stress of the final exam flunks out.

There is the driver who all of his life has had a flawless record, and then, in a moment of carelessness, is involved in a tragic accident.

There is the trusted employee whose performance has been excellent, and then he succumbs to the temptation to steal a little from his employer. A mark is placed on him that never entirely disappears.

There is the life lived with decency—and then comes the destructive, ever-haunting, one-time moral letdown.

There is the outburst of anger that suddenly destroys a long-cherished relationship.

In all of these, someone has "dropped the ball." Someone failed to be true to himself, true to his team, true to what he knew to be right, true to his internal code of ethics and morality.

Athens, Greece, was once recognized as the great and unique city of the world. Each young man of Athens, when he reached the age of seventeen, took this oath:

> We will never bring disgrace on this our City by an act of dishonesty or cowardice.
> We will fight for the ideals and sacred things of the City, both alone and with many.
> We will revere and obey the City's laws, and will do our best to incite a like reverence and respect in those above us who are prone to annul them or set them at naught.
> We will strive increasingly to quicken the public sense of civic duty.
> Thus in all these ways we will transmit this City, not only less, but greater and more beautiful than it was transmitted to us.

That solemn commitment on the part of the young men of Athens became the foundation of principle and behavior that made Athens the cultural capital of the world.

Imagine what would happen in our countries, in our families, in our places of business, in our cities and towns if every young man and woman took and honored such an oath today. The results would be spectacular!

Be true to what is right and fair and honest. Lend your strength to crusading against things that tear down the character of men and women. Stand up for integrity in your classrooms, among your peers, in your homes and families, and in the society of which you are an important part. Your strong voice is needed. The weight of your stance may be enough to tip the scales in the direction of truth.

Be true to your parents and your heritage. Regrettably there are a few parents who behave in a way that does serious injustice to their children.

But these cases are relatively few. No one has a greater interest in your happiness than do your mothers and fathers. They were once your age. Your problems are not substantially different from what theirs were. If they occasionally place restrictions on you, it is because they see danger in the road ahead. Listen to them. What they ask you to do may not be to your liking. But you will be much happier if you do it.

Be true to others and to yourself by telling the truth. Become known as someone who is unfailingly honest. Don't ever cheat. How would you like to have an operation on which your life depended done by a doctor who had cheated his way through medical school? It's better to fail than to cheat.

Be true to the truth! How cheaply some men and women sell their good names! Among many unsigned letters I have received was one that contained a twenty-dollar bill and a brief note that stated that the writer had come to my home many years ago. When there had been no response to the bell, he had tried the door and, finding it unlocked, had entered and walked about. On the dresser he had seen a twenty-dollar bill. He had taken it and had then left undetected. Through the years his conscience had bothered him, and he was now returning the money.

He did not include anything for interest for the period during which he had used the money. But as I read his pathetic letter I thought of the usury to which he had subjected himself for a quarter of a century with the unceasing nagging of his conscience. For him there had been no peace until he had made restitution.

Be true. Be true to your own convictions. You know what is right, and you know what is wrong. You know when you are doing the proper thing. You know when you are giving strength to the right cause. Be loyal. Be faithful. Be true.

6

BE POSITIVE

S IXTH, BE POSITIVE ABOUT YOUR LIFE.

Nearly every day I glance through several papers. I like to know what is happening in the world. And when I have time, I listen to the commentators on television and radio. These writers and commentators are intelligent. These men and women are masters of the spoken and written word. But for the most part, their attitude is negative and derogatory. They seem unable to deal with balanced truth, notwithstanding their loud protests to the contrary. They feed us a steady and sour diet of character assassination, faultfinding, and evil speaking of one another that caricatures the facts and distorts the truth. Regardless of whom they write or speak about, they seem to look for his or her failings or weaknesses. They constantly criticize and seldom praise.

This spirit of negativism is not limited to columnists and commentators. Read the letters to the editor in your local paper. You will find that many are filled with venom, written by people who seem to find no good in the world. To hear tell, there is nowhere a man or woman of integrity holding political office. Yes, from time to time some of our leaders disappoint us. But there are many men and women serving with honor and integrity. This spirit of animosity has infected all of us to a certain degree. We see it in the sitcoms on television. We hear it in the hallways at school. We hear it in the way we talk to each other. In our homes some youth eventually give up under the barrage of constant criticism leveled by their parents. The snide remark, the sarcastic jibe, the cutting down of others—these too often are the essence of our conversation. Faultfinding, evil speaking, and criticizing each other as we comment on each other's lives and choices—these are the spirit of the day, I am sorry to say. In our homes, there is far too much criticism. Criticism is the forerunner of divorce, the cultivator of rebellion, and sometimes a catalyst that leads to failure.

I would like to suggest that we stop seeking out the storms of life and enjoy the sunlight. I am suggesting that we "accentuate the positive." I am asking that we look a little deeper for the good, that we still our voices of insult and sarcasm, that we more generously compliment virtue and hard effort. There is good all around us—if we will only look for it.

I am not suggesting that all criticism be silenced. Growth comes of correction. Strength comes of repentance. I am not suggesting that our conversation be all honey. Wise is the young man or young woman who can acknowledge mistakes and become better as a result.

But I am suggesting that we look for the great good among those with whom we associate and live, that we speak of one another's virtues and positive qualities more than we speak of one another's faults, that optimism replace pessimism, and that our faith exceed our fears. When I was a young man and tended to be critical of others, my wise father would often say, "Cynics do not contribute, skeptics do not create, doubters do not achieve." Who wants to be around someone who is always forecasting doom? Who wants to be fed a steady diet of the negative? Optimism, on the other hand, and looking on the bright side, refreshes everyone.

In my ninety-plus years, I have learned a secret. I have learned that when good men and good women face challenges with optimism, things will always work out! Truly, things always work out! Despite how difficult circumstances may look at the moment, those who have faith and move forward with a happy spirit will find that things always work out.

If ever there was a man who demonstrated this, it was the prime minister of England during World War II, Winston Churchill. The year 1940 was a desperate time when bombs were falling on London. The German war machine had overrun much of Europe and was moving into Russia. Most of Europe was in the dread grasp of tyranny, and England was to be next. In that dangerous hour, when the hearts of men were failing, and when fear gripped everyone, Churchill spoke, saying,

> Do not let us speak of darker days; let us speak rather of sterner days. These are not dark days; these are great days—the greatest days our country has ever lived and we must all thank God that we have been allowed, each of us according to our stations, to play a part in making these days memorable in the history of our race.

Following the terrible catastrophe of the defeat of Dunkirk, the prophets of doom foretold the end of Britain. But in that dark and solemn hour, more than sixty years ago, I heard this remarkable man say as his words were broadcast across America:

We shall not fail . . . we shall fight in France, we shall fight on the seas and oceans, we shall fight with growing confidence and growing strength in the air, we shall defend our island, whatever the cost may be. We shall fight on the beaches, we shall fight on the landing grounds, we shall fight in the fields and in the streets, we shall fight in the hills; we shall never surrender. (Speech on Dunkirk, House of Commons, 4 June 1940.)

It was this kind of talk, which saw a ray of sunlight through the horrible gloom, that saved the British from bitter defeat.

Years ago I read a column by Sydney Harris that said that Sir Walter Scott and Lord Byron both caused trouble at school. Thomas Edison was considered dumb. Burns and Boccaccio did poorly in school. Thomas Aquinas, who was later thought to have perhaps the finest scholastic mind among Catholic thinkers, was labeled "the dumb ox" at school. Sir Issac Newton was last in his class. Each of these men was later hailed as a genius.

I imagine that most of you will be underestimated at some point in your life. And I am sure that each of you will have difficulties ahead of you. None of us can avoid them. But do not despair. Do not give up. They will not last forever. Look for the sunlight in the clouds. God will not forsake you.

I am grateful for the words of a favorite hymn:

When upon life's billows
   you are tempest-tossed,
When you are discouraged,
   thinking all is lost,
Count your many blessings;
   name them one by one,
And it will surprise you
   what the Lord has done. . . .

So amid the conflict,
   whether great or small

Do not be discouraged;
    God is over all.
Count your many blessings;
    angels will attend,
Help and comfort give you
    to your journey's end.
    ("Count Your Blessings," *Hymns*, no. 241)

My dear friends, in whom I have such confidence, don't partake of the spirit of our times. Don't always be looking for the dark side of life. Look for the good. There is so much of the sweet and the decent and the positive to build upon.

Cultivate an attitude of optimism. Know that God is watching over you, that He will hear your prayers and will answer them, that He loves you and will make that love manifest.

7

BE HUMBLE

S EVENTH, BE HUMBLE.

　　When I was a young man in my early twenties I served a mission for my church. I was sent to England, and the first city in which I lived was Preston, Lancashire. Because of the Depression, money was scarce. If a man had a job making fifty dollars a month, he considered himself fortunate. I left people who were poor to go and preach to people who were also poor.

　　Before traveling to England, I had never before seen the ocean. Going to the British Isles was, therefore, a grand adventure. I loved England, but in those days there were very few people who were interested in talking about religion. My companion and I had doors slammed in our faces. Dogs ran after us and barked at our heels. And to make matters worse, the lush, green countryside of

England played havoc with my hay fever. My eyes and nose began to run the minute I stepped foot in England, and I was miserable.

For all of these reasons, after a short time in Preston, and realizing that my being gone from home was a hardship on my family, I wrote my father saying that I was wasting his money and my time, and that I ought to come home than rather than stay the two years I was scheduled to be there.

His reply soon came, and it was short and to the point: "Dear Gordon. I have your letter of such and such a date. I have only one suggestion—forget yourself and go to work."

About the same day I received that letter, I happened to read this verse in the New Testament: "He that findeth his life shall lose it: and he that loseth his life for my sake shall find it" (Matthew 10:39). I can remember getting on my knees and pleading for forgiveness for my selfish attitude. Between my father's letter and that verse of scripture, I made a resolution that changed my attitude and outlook on life. I can trace everything good that has happened to me back to that singular decision to forget myself and go to work.

Be humble. Don't be arrogant. The world is full of arrogant people. How obnoxious they are! There is no place for arrogance in our lives. There is no place for conceit. There is no place for egotism. I believe that if we are without conceit and pride and arrogance, then we can ask God to lead us by the hand. What greater thing could we ask for?

I believe that you—yes, you—can make a difference in the world. It may be ever so small, but it will count for the greater good.

I first read the following words some seventy years ago in a college English class:

> What a piece of work is a man! how noble in reason! how infinite in faculty! in form and moving how express and admirable! in action how like an angel! in apprehension how like a god! (*Hamlet*, II. ii. 303–6)

I recognize that these words of Hamlet were spoken in irony. And yet there is so much of truth in them. They describe the great potential excellence of men and women. They go hand in hand with these words of David:

> When I consider thy heavens, the work of thy fingers, the moon and the stars, which thou hast ordained; What is man, that thou art mindful of him? And the son of man that thou visitest him? For thou hast made him a little lower than the angels, and hast crowned him with glory and honour (Psalms 8:3–5).

These magnificent words declare the wonder of man, of each of us. We are more than a son or daughter of Mr. and Mrs. So-and-So who reside in such-and-such a place. We are all children of God, and there is something of divinity within each of us.

It is precisely because we understand our divine heritage and potential that we ought to be humble about who we are. Being humble does not mean being weak. It means being teachable. It does not require us to be trampled upon. It means acknowledging where our strengths and abilities come from. It also means recognizing that we are not here on earth to see how important we can become, but to see how much difference we can make in the lives of others.

Not long ago I picked up an old book and read about the life of Florence Nightingale. Though I had read this book before, my re-reading brought a new sense of admiration and respect for this great young English woman who made such a tremendous difference in her time.

She was born to the upper class, to party and to dance, to go to horse races and look pretty in society. But she was interested in none of it. Her parents could not understand her. Even when she was young, her great desire was to alleviate pain and suffering, to hasten healing, to make less dreadful the hospitals of the day. She never married. She devoted her life to nursing, and she became expert at it.

In 1854, Britain was embroiled in the Crimean War. Miss Nightingale had friends at the head of the government, and she relentlessly pursued and persuaded them until she was appointed director of the hospital in Scutari, where thousands of the victims of the war were brought.

The picture that greeted her there was one of absolute despair and dismay. An old warehouse served as a hospital. The sanitary conditions were deplorable. Wounded men were crowded in great rooms that reeked of foul odors and the cries of the suffering.

This fragile looking young woman set to work. Her biographer wrote this:

> For those who watched her at work among the sick, moving day and night from bed to bed, with that unflinching courage, with indefatigable vigilance, it seems as if the concentrated force of an undivided and unparalleled devotion could hardly suffice for that first portion of her task alone. Wherever, in those vast wards suffering was at its worst and the need

for help was greatest, there, as if by magic, was Miss Nightingale. (Lytton Strachey, *Life of Florence Nightingale*, Travelers Library, Doubleday, Doran & Co., 1934.)

The beds that held the suffering men literally stretched for miles, with barely space between each bed to walk. But somehow, within a period of six months,

> The confusion and the pressure in the wards had come to an end; order reigned in them, and cleanliness; the supplies were bountiful and prompt; important sanitary works had been carried out. One comparison of figures was enough to reveal the extraordinary change: the rate of mortality among the cases treated had fallen from 42 percent to 22 per thousand. (Ibid., p. 1186.)

Florence Nightingale had brought to pass an absolute miracle. Lives by the thousands were saved. Men who had no hope were given hope.

The war ended. She might have gone back to London a heroine. The public press had sung her praise. But she returned incognito to escape the adulation. She continued her work for another 50 years, improving the hospitals of England, both military and civilian.

Perhaps no other woman in the history of the world has done so much to reduce human misery as this lady with the lamp, who walked through the vast wards of Scutari in the middle of the nineteenth century, spreading cheer and comfort, faith and hope to those who writhed in pain. She had been born to privilege. Instead, she lived a life of excellence because of her profound humility, which created within her the desire to serve and help others.

To you who have your lives ahead of you, I make a plea—that with all of your getting and going and doing, you will also give something to make the world a little better.

One day in the Dallas airport a man walked up to me and introduced himself. He was a medical doctor on his way to Central America. Each year he goes there for a month to perform numerous operations to help those who are unable to pay for the kind of assistance he can give.

Would you resolve today to dedicate a part of your life to those in distress and need? Doing this will help you keep your feet on the ground. It will help you resist the temptation to think that somehow the world owes you something. It will keep you humble.

Be Humble! Recognize that everything you have—your time, your talents and skills, your health and energy, your accomplishments, and your very lives—come as free gifts from your Father in Heaven. How grateful we ought to be for His goodness to us. How humble we ought to be to think that He knows who we are, and that He is waiting to guide our every step.

8

BE STILL

EIGHTH, BE STILL.

The world is so noisy. There are voices everywhere trying to influence us. We all need time to think. We need to drown out the clamor and noise and simply be quiet. We need time to ponder and meditate, and to contemplate the deeper things of life. We need time to read and to immerse ourselves in the thoughts of great minds.

Our lives are so busy. We run from one thing to another. We wear ourselves out with our studies and our social lives and our pursuit of money. Please don't misunderstand me: I am not saying that any of these things are wrong or bad. But we are entitled to spend some time with ourselves. We need to spend time out in nature where we can think and breathe deeply and feel the earth and listen to the sounds of the ocean or the woods or the mountains.

I can vividly picture my father as he began to age. He lived in a home where there was a rock wall on the grounds. It was a low wall, and when the weather was warm, he would go and sit on his wall. When I was a young man, I wondered why my father would just sit on this wall for hours at a time. He would think and meditate and ponder things to say and write, for he was a gifted speaker and writer. But even in his old age, he read voraciously. He never ceased growing. Life was for him a great adventure in thinking and reading.

Both my father and mother were educators, and in my boyhood home they built a large library filled with books. In that room was a large table where we could study with good lamps for reading. As a young boy, I found constant excuses for avoiding homework. But I liked to read, and the emphasis my parents placed on reading finally caught up with me. I have loved to read ever since.

A man I know who is driven by much pressure and responsibility said to me on one occasion, "If only I had time to read a good book." He could make time. Establish that pattern now. Read, study, and ponder so that you will continue doing so throughout your life.

Your desires along these lines will vary with your age and circumstances. But all of us need some of it. I ask you to think about all of the time you spend in front of your computer, maybe surfing the Internet, or plugged in to video games, or watching some of the inane programs and sports contests on television. I am not anti-sports. I enjoy a good football or basketball game. But I have seen so many men and women become addicted to sports or the Internet or video games. I know far too many people who are controlled by the noise and opinions they have constantly coming into their lives and minds. I believe their lives would be richer and more rewarding if at least occasionally they would get up from watching a game that will be forgotten tomorrow, get up from surfing one more web site, and spend a little time reading and thinking and simply Being Still.

They would be blessed if they would occasionally ride out into the darkness at night, look at the stars, and ponder their place in the world.

Find some time to drown out the noise of the world. Find your own version of a rock wall and take occasion to think about your life. Take time to think about the kind of man or woman you want to become.

The scriptures admonish: "Be still, and know that I am God" (Psalm 46:10).

9
BE PRAYERFUL

FINALLY, BE PRAYERFUL.

You cannot do it alone. I know that around the world are young people from all walks of life who pray. I know there are many of you who get on your knees and speak with God. You know that He is the source of all wisdom.

You need His help, and you know that you need His help. You cannot do it alone. You will come to realize that and recognize it more and more as the years pass. Live so that in good conscience you can speak with God. Get on your knees and thank Him for His goodness to you and express to Him the righteous desires of your hearts. The miracle of it all is that He hears. He responds. He answers—not always as we might wish He would answer, but there is no question or doubt in my mind that He answers.

I learned this, too, as a boy.

The fruit farm on which we lived in the summer was in the country where the nights were
dark. There were no streetlights or anything of
that kind to illuminate any of the surrounding
area. My brother and I often slept out-of-doors.
On clear nights, we would lie on our backs and
look at the myriads of stars in the heavens.
We could identify some of the constellations
and other stars as they were illustrated in our en-
cyclopedia. Each night we would trace the Big
Dipper, the handle and the cup, to find the
North Star.

We came to know of the constancy of that
star. As the earth turned, the others appeared to
move through the night. But the North Star held
its position in line with the axis of the earth. And
so it had come to be known as the Polar Star, or
the Polestar, or the Lodestar. Through centuries of
time, mariners had used it to guide them in their
journeys. They had reckoned their bearings by its
constancy, thereby avoiding traveling in circles or

in the wrong direction, as they moved across the wide, unmarked seas.

Because of those boyhood musings, the Polar Star came to mean something to me. I recognized it is a constant in the midst of change. It is something that can always be counted on, something that is dependable, an anchor in what otherwise appeared to be a moving and unstable firmament.

May I suggest to you that prayer can become like the Polar Star in your life. In a changing and sometimes misleading and discouraging world, it can be a constant. Communicating with your Heavenly Father through prayer can give you a feeling of security. It can bless you with peace and comfort and wisdom. It can result in direction and guidance.

My parents taught us to pray. We learned how to go before our Heavenly Father and talk with Him about our concerns and worries. We learned also to thank Him daily for all that He did for us. And then came the day in my life when I began to really understand how powerful prayer can be.

From the time I was young, I knew that my father loved my mother. He encouraged her in every way. Her comfort was his constant concern. As children, we looked upon our parents as equals, companions who worked together and loved and appreciated one another. Knowing that our parents deeply loved each other brought us a sense of security.

At the age of fifty, my mother developed cancer. I recall our family prayers, with our tearful pleadings. My father did everything he could to get mother the treatment she needed, including sending her to the best specialist that could be found on the West Coast, but to no avail. I still remember vividly the day my brokenhearted father returned from Los Angeles after mother had died. He stepped off the train and greeted his grief-stricken children. We walked solemnly down the station platform to the baggage car, where the casket was unloaded. We came to know even more about the tenderness of our father's heart. I also came to know something of heartache and loss— the absolute devastation of children losing their mother—but also of peace without pain and the certainty that death cannot be the end of the soul.

We didn't speak openly about love for one another very much in those days. But we prayed together. We prayed for comfort and strength and understanding. We prayed for peace. We prayed for our mother who had gone on before us. We prayed that we would be able to live up to the legacy she had left us. We prayed that our father's heart would heal, and that our Heavenly Father would heal our broken hearts and make us stronger. We felt the quiet strength that comes to families who pray together.

None of us can do it alone. Without help you cannot possibly enjoy the success for which you dream. I know from personal experience that God will pour down wisdom and a feeling of peace upon the heads of those who get on their knees and speak with Him.

I repeat, You need His help, and you know that you need His help. Not only can you not do it alone, but you need not try to do it alone. There will be times when it does not seem that the answers to your prayers are forthcoming. But the Lord is wiser than we are. He will always hear our prayers, and He will always answer them.

I worked many years with a man whom I loved to hear pray because his prayers were almost entirely filled with giving thanks rather than asking for things.

The marvelous thing about prayer is that it is personal, it is individual, it is private in terms of your speaking with your Father in Heaven. Ask God to forgive your sins. Ask Him to bless you. Ask Him to help you realize your righteous and worthy ambitions. Ask Him to help you with your studies. Ask Him to take away your worries and fears. Ask Him to help you find a companion with whom you can share your life. Ask Him for all of the things that mean so much to you. He stands ready to help because we are His sons and daughters. Don't ever forget that.

When I was interviewed by Mike Wallace for CBS's 60 Minutes program, he asked me this question: "People speak of you as a prophet. Does God talk to you?" I responded by telling him that a prophet isn't a fortune-teller. It is more likely to be as it was when Elijah called on the Lord for help and the scripture says there was a great wind, and the Lord was not in the wind. There was an earthquake and the Lord was not in the earthquake. There was fire, and after the fire a still small voice. It is the voice of the Spirit which speaks, and which will speak to you concerning your own problems, if you will seek for wisdom and understanding in prayer.

George Washington believed in prayer. A friend of Washington by the name of Potts was present with General Washington and his young army at Valley Forge during the terrible winter of 1777. One day walking along a path, Potts could hear the sound of someone speaking very earnestly. As he approached the area from which the sound was coming, he found George Washington, the commander in chief of the American armies, on his knees in prayer, pleading with the heavens on behalf of his troops. This man Potts returned to his home and told his wife that all was going to be well, adding this:

> I have this day seen what I never expected. Thee knows that I always thought the sword and the gospel utterly inconsistent; and that no man could be soldier and a Christian at the same time. But George Washington has this day convinced me of my mistake. (From Mason Locke Weems, *Life of Washington*, Armonk, NY: M. E. Sharpe, 1986, p. 147.)

Prayer will change your life. It will bring you peace. It will give you direction and guidance. It will help you feel that you are not alone in this big and sometimes brutal world. The Lord answers our prayers. I know that. I have seen it happen again and again and again.

I recall reading about William Robert Anderson, who took the submarine *Nautilus* under the North Pole. He carried in his wallet a dog-eared card on which were written these words:

> I believe I am always divinely guided. I believe I will always take the right road. I believe God will always make a way where there is no way.

So do I. I too believe that God will make a way, will open a window, will show us a road even when it seems there is nowhere to turn. I hope that every young man and young woman will get on his or her knees night and morning and speak with the Lord. We can be perfect in our prayers.

CONCLUSION

This is a time to be happy. This is a time to feel joy and make friends and enjoy the best this life has to offer. What I have tried to put forth in this little book are simply a few suggestions, gained from many years of living, to help you do just that. The world will tell you that certain kinds of things will bring you happiness—things such as popularity and possessions and satisfying your baser desires.

You have such a tremendous responsibility, you young men and young women. You are the products of all of the generations that have gone before you. All that you have of body and mind has been passed to you through your parents. Someday you will become parents and pass on to succeeding generations the qualities of body and mind which you have received from the past. Do not break the chain of the generations of your family. Keep it bright and strong. So very much depends on you. You are so very precious.

You can have a good time. Of course you can! I want you to have fun. I want you to enjoy your life. I do not want you to be prudes. I want you to be robust and cheerful, to sing and dance, to laugh and be happy.

But in so doing, be humble and prayerful, and the smiles of heaven will fall upon you.

I could wish for you nothing better than that your lives be fruitful, that your service be dedicated and freely given, that you contribute to the knowledge and the well-being of the world in which you live, and that you do it humbly and faithfully before your God. He loves you. I love you. I believe in you. And I want you to be happy and successful, to make significant contributions to the world.

These, then are my nine Be's.

Be Grateful.

Be Smart.

Be Involved.

Be Clean.

Be True.

Be Positive.

Be Humble.

Be Still.

Be Prayerful.

There they are, nine Be's which, if observed, will bring handsome dividends to any young man or woman. They will add sparkle to your days and peace to your nights. They will save you from heartache and pain. They will bring purpose into your life and give direction to your energies.

They will bring you friends of your own kind. They will protect you from associations that would pull you down and deflect you from your course.

Never forget that you have far more years ahead of you than you have behind you. Those years can be productive and rewarding. The good things of which you dream in your better moments will become realities.

If today you find yourself only drifting as a leaf in a stream, get hold of yourself and determine you will do better.

At railroad grade crossings, signs of warning were once common. Two cross arms were emblazoned with the words, "Stop, Look, Listen." They meant that a train could be roaring down the tracks, and you had better be alert.

I was riding a train in the Midwest years ago. I looked out the window to my left. A road ran parallel to the tracks. A car with a boy and a girl was speeding down the road a little faster than the train. The car moved ahead until I could no longer see it. Suddenly, the locomotive whistle sounded and the train screeched to a halt as the brakes gripped the wheels.

We looked out the window on the other side. There was a mangled car. Police cars soon converged, followed by an ambulance. The boy and girl were both dead.

The road they were traveling crossed the tracks. They did not stop, look, or listen. It all happened in an instant.

The better way to Be is the way of these nine Be's.

The years will inevitably pass, and pass quickly. Today is your day of resolution. Promise yourself to make something good of the precious life that God has given you.